BIG SPORTS BRANDS

BURTON

Peak Snowboard Producer

by Paul D. Bowker

SportsZone

An Imprint of Abdo Publishing
abdobooks.com

abdobooks.com

Published by Abdo Publishing, a division of ABDO, PO Box 398166, Minneapolis, Minnesota 55439. Copyright © 2024 by Abdo Consulting Group, Inc. International copyrights reserved in all countries. No part of this book may be reproduced in any form without written permission from the publisher. SportsZone™ is a trademark and logo of Abdo Publishing.

Printed in the United States of America, North Mankato, Minnesota.
052023
092023

Cover Photo: Tim Clayton/Corbis Sport/Getty Images
Interior Photos: Brian Bahr/Getty Images Sport/Getty Images, 4–5; Andrey Artykov/ Alamy, 7; Michael Loccisano/FilmMagic/Getty Images, 9; jackrcoyne/Stockimo/Alamy, 10–11; Alden Pellett/AP Images, 12; Mark Galloway/Stockimo/Alamy, 13; Jesse Lirola/ Getty Images for Burton Snowboards/Getty Images Entertainment/Getty Images, 14; Ben Blankenburg/Keystone Resort/AP Images, 16; John Lamparski/Getty Images Sport/Getty Images, 18–19; Ken Hively/Los Angeles Times/Getty Images, 21; Justin Sullivan/Getty Images News/Getty Images, 22; Bryan Bedder/Getty Images for Burton Snowboards/Getty Images Entertainment/Getty Images, 25; Emmanuel Dunand/AFP/ Getty Images, 26–27; Gregory Bull/AP Images, 29; Al Bello/Getty Images Sport/Getty Images, 30; Sean M. Haffey/Getty Images Sport/Getty Images, 31; Christopher Polk/ Getty Images for Burton/Getty Images Entertainment/Getty Images, 32, 39; Melih Evren/ Shutterstock Images, 34–35; Shutterstock Images, 36; Johannes Kroemer/Getty Images Entertainment/Getty Images, 41

Editors: Steph Giedd and Priscilla An
Series Designer: Joshua Olson

Library of Congress Control Number: 2022949055

Publisher's Cataloging-in-Publication Data

Names: Bowker, Paul D., author.
Title: Burton: peak snowboard producer / by Paul D. Bowker
Other title: peak snowboard producer
Description: Minneapolis, Minnesota: Abdo Publishing Company, 2024 | Series: Big sports brands | Includes online resources and index.
Identifiers: ISBN 9781098290665 (lib. bdg.) | ISBN 9781098276843 (ebook)
Subjects: LCSH: Snowboards--Juvenile literature. | Sports--Equipment and supplies--Juvenile literature. | Brand name products--Juvenile literature. | Snowboards--Juvenile literature. | Winter sports--Juvenile literature.
Classification: DDC 658.827--dc23

TABLE OF CONTENTS

Chapter One

SNOWBOARDING MAGIC

Snowboarder Kelly Clark attacked the half-pipe in her first Olympic Games in 2002 in Salt Lake City, Utah. On her second run of the finals, Clark put together one of the best performances of her career. She performed seven tricks, including a 540-degree spin. Later in the run, Clark landed a challenging trick called a McTwist. And finally, she ended her great run by nailing a 720.

Clark raised her arms above her head, and the crowd cheered. At just 18 years old, she had clinched her first Olympic gold medal. No US snowboarder had done that before.

Kelly Clark performs a trick using her Burton snowboard during the 2002 Winter Olympics qualifying rounds.

Clark proudly held up her Burton snowboard after her winning run. She was already part of the Burton snowboarding team. When Clark won her gold medal, Burton founder Jake Burton Carpenter was there to watch the moment in person.

Clark went on to compete in five Olympic Winter Games during her career and won three medals. She was the first athlete to compete in 19 consecutive Winter X Games. In addition, she was the first female snowboarder to land a 1,080-degree spin in a half-pipe competition. She accomplished all those feats on Burton snowboards. When Clark retired in 2019, she had been endorsing Burton for 20 years.

Equal Sharing

Burton supports inclusivity for women and girls in leadership and athletics. In 2004 Burton founder Jake Burton Carpenter and his wife, Donna, created the Women's Leadership Initiative, which creates more leadership opportunities for women within Burton. For example, senior leadership in the company is shared 50-50 by men and women. Since it began in 1982, the Burton US Open awards equal prize money to women and men.

Building a Business

When Carpenter founded the company in 1977, the prospects for a brand like Burton seemed almost nonexistent. Snowboarding was not a recognized sport. Many ski resorts didn't even allow snowboarders on their slopes.

This display at the Holmenkollen Ski Museum in Norway shows how snowboards used to look.

As snowboarding gained widespread acceptance, Burton skyrocketed in popularity. Since then, Burton has evolved into a brand recognized around the world. In 2022 Burton had 600 employees with offices in six countries. And in that year alone, it had $260 million in revenue.

Burton's primary business was making snowboards. But the company has branched out into making apparel such as winter jackets and snow pants. It also sells a variety of products including backpacks and coolers. However, the company is still grounded in the sport of snowboarding. Burton sells snowboards and goggles that are created with the newest technology.

Along the way, Burton has created one of the biggest competitions for snowboarders, the Burton US Open. It is the longest-running yearly snowboarding event. Snowboard legends including Shaun White and Kelly Clark have made their marks by winning multiple events there.

Those athletes are also two of many prominent snowboarders Burton has sponsored over the years. These endorsement deals help Burton stay at the forefront of the sport. Burton products and events continue to influence the culture of snowboarding.

Started in 1982, the Burton US Open has grown into one of the biggest snowboarding competitions in the world.

Chapter Two

NEW ERA OF SNOWBOARDING

In 1965 Michigan businessman Sherman Poppen invented the Snurfer. This was the first version of what became known as a snowboard. The Snurfer was first made by binding two children's skis together. It later became a wooden board with a rope attached to it. The rope helped the rider steer. When the board hit the market, it immediately became popular. The sport eventually became called snowboarding after Poppen trademarked the term "Snurfer."

In 1968 Jake Burton Carpenter bought a Snurfer for $10. He spent hours Snurfing in the snow. This wasn't

The name Snurfer was created by joining the words "snow" and "surf."

his first experience with snow. Carpenter had spent his childhood skiing with his family. He enjoyed the ski trips even more because he knew that it meant no school.

In 1970 Carpenter was expelled from boarding school for being part of a prank. That same year, Carpenter started attending another prep school, the Marvelwood School in Connecticut. He decided to take his second chance in school seriously. Carpenter graduated at the top of his class. While in his last semester of high school, he moved to New York for an independent study program. During that time, Carpenter started his own landscaping business.

After graduating from high school, Carpenter attended the University of Colorado Boulder for a year. Then he transferred to New York University (NYU) and studied economics. Carpenter was also the captain of the school's swim team.

Jake Burton Carpenter shows off his prototype snowboard, *right*, which has a rope handle attached to the nose of the board.

Burton is the number one snowboard manufacturer in the world.

He graduated from NYU in 1977 and worked in an investment banking firm. However, Carpenter grew tired of the long hours. Some days he worked as long as 12 to 14 hours. Though years had passed, he was still thinking about Snurfing.

Carpenter was confident that snowboarding had the potential to become a recognized sport. Using a saber saw in his Manhattan apartment, he crafted one of his first snowboards out of wood. Carpenter then decided to start a snowboarding company, so he drew up a business plan.

Donna, Carpenter's wife, *left*, was Burton's CEO from 2016 to 2020.

The plan was based on making 50 snowboards a day. That would allow him to make $100,000 in salary each year. Carpenter quit his job and moved to Londonderry, Vermont. There, he started making Burton Boards inside a barn. At first, he began making boards as a plan to get rich quickly. However, his business was not very successful at first. Nobody was buying his product because snowboarding was not a widely known sport. His business model was not going to plan.

Snowboarding was not an Olympic sport, so Carpenter soon became passionate about making snowboarding a sport. There were no snowboard runs at ski resorts as there are now.

While starting Burton Boards, Carpenter was a live-in caretaker. He also took care of two horses. On top of that, Carpenter worked as a bartender at night at the Birkenhaus Inn. During the day, he made and sold snowboards. He tested the boards on the snowy hills of southern Vermont. In the beginning, it was a slow start to get his business off the ground.

After selling his 700th board, Carpenter started finding increased success. In 1981 he moved to Manchester, Vermont. He bought his first house there. The house had a barn, which became the factory. His living room was the store. Carpenter's basement was converted into a snowboard warehouse, and his bedroom became the office. On New Year's Eve in 1981, Carpenter met Donna Gaston. They eventually married in 1983. In the following years, Donna would become an essential part of the Burton business.

Going Global

In 1984 the Carpenters went to Austria for a ski trip with Donna's parents. For Jake, it was more than just a trip. In the daytime, he snowboarded while the rest of the family skied. In the evening, he visited ski manufacturers.

One late night, he managed to find the owner of Keil Ski, a manufacturer in Uttendorf, Austria. The owner did not speak English, so he had to wake up his daughter to translate.

Snowboarding became popular in the 1980s and 1990s. This Keystone Resort ski patroller makes his way down a run on the first day snowboarders were allowed at the resort in 1996.

Carpenter and the owner shook hands at midnight and created a business partnership. Soon Carpenter and Keil Ski produced a prototype. It was displayed at a show in Las Vegas, Nevada. Hermann Kapferer, a businessman from Innsbruck, Austria, personally brought the board to Las Vegas. Kapferer later helped Carpenter establish a facility in Innsbruck.

In 1985 the Carpenters moved to a town near Innsbruck. Burton Europe was born. Donna ran the operation and became the company's chief financial officer in 1989. Kapferer became general manager. Innsbruck was already a winter sports city after hosting the 1964 and 1976 Olympic Winter Games. But snowboarding changed Innsbruck. "The city of Innsbruck got a whole new image after Burton settled there: the traditional mountain town became a lot more young, dynamic, and trend-setting," said Kapferer.

Booming Business

Sales grew significantly for Burton in the 1980s and 1990s. In 1986 Burton snowboards and gear could be found at more than 1,000 retail shops in the United States. In 1992 Carpenter moved the business again. The company settled in Burlington, a city in northern Vermont. By then, Burton had expanded to more than 100 employees.

During the 1980s and 1990s, snowboarding grew even more popular. Ski resorts in the United States, which had once prohibited snowboarders, were now welcoming them. Then, in 1998, snowboarding got a massive boost when it was included in the Olympic Winter Games for the first time in Nagano, Japan. Carpenter's vision of making snowboarding a sport finally became reality. But that was just the beginning for the Burton brand.

Sno-Boarding?

When snowboarding made its debut in the 1998 Olympic Winter Games in Nagano, Japan, Burton founder Jake Burton Carpenter was excited. But when he arrived at the venue in Japan, he saw a sign that stated: Sno-Boarding. "It was not a cool moment at all," Carpenter said.

Chapter Three

BOARDS AND BEYOND

Burton got its start by making snowboards, but the company didn't stop there. Since Burton's beginnings, Jake Burton Carpenter was all about improving snowboarding for athletes. Carpenter's relationships with snowboarders made up an important part of the company's vision. Burton products expanded as the company worked to cater more toward athletes and their needs.

Craig Kelly was a well-known freerider around the world. He won four world championships in the late 1980s and early 1990s. In 1989 Kelly and Burton

Jake Burton Carpenter, *in orange*, poses with US Olympic snowboarders, *from left*, Chloe Kim, Kelly Clark, and Danny Davis at a Burton event in 2017.

partnered to create the Mystery Air board. The next year, Kelly signed a long-term deal with Burton. Kelly and Carpenter became close friends. Carpenter credits Kelly with getting him to listen closely to snowboarders. After Kelly died in 2003 in an avalanche while training to become a Canadian mountain guide near Revelstoke, British Columbia, Carpenter designed a Mine Craig Kelly jacket and shirt to honor his friend. In 2011, when Burton opened a lab for research and development, it was named Craig's Prototype Facility.

Chilling Out

The Chill Foundation was founded in 1995 by Jake and Donna Carpenter. The foundation is based in Burlington, Vermont. It has served more than 3,000 youth in multiple countries each year. The foundation works with a number of social service agencies, mental health agencies, foster care programs, juvenile justice programs, and schools.

Giving back to the community is important to Burton Snowboards. One way the company does that is through their Chill Foundation, which gives opportunities to underserved youth to build self-esteem and life skills through board sports. In the 2010s, Carpenter collaborated with artist Jeff Koons to help the Chill Foundation. They designed a snowboard called the Philosopher, which was released in 2016. The design included graphics based on the cave from the ancient book Plato's *Republic*. Only 50 boards

Burton's first retail store in Los Angeles is located in West Hollywood.

were produced. These boards carried a purchase price of $5,000. Proceeds from those sales were a benefit for the Chill Foundation.

New Technology

Looking to improve their snowboards, Burton engineers reached out to the National Aeronautics and Space Administration (NASA). They wanted to find out more about the "honeycomb" process. NASA had used that process to produce material that was lighter and stronger for space travel.

When NASA declined to share the technology, Burton's experts went to work. After the design work was done, Burton

In 2005 Burton unveiled a new collection that infused Bluetooth technology with apparel, including beanies.

patented its product. NASA gained interest when they saw that the new honeycomb process was better than the one NASA's engineers had come up with.

With the new technology, Burton created an innovative board called the Vapor. It was more expensive than most boards, costing approximately $1,200. But for advanced snowboarders, the price was worth the outcome.

The Vapor was an example of the many innovations and trends that Burton has made. Burton's plaid-style clothing was copied by other manufacturers. Burton also hired a Japanese designer, Hiroshi Fujiwara, to come up with a successful clothing line. When iPods came along, Burton designed jackets with a built-in iPod control pad in the arm of the jacket. This made changing songs easier so that snowboarders didn't have to fumble with zippers or take off their gloves to change their music.

Burton started a brand called Anon Optics in 2001. Anon's purpose is to create stylish and effective snowboarding and ski goggles. It also sells helmets and accessories, including face masks and sunglasses. The brand became known for its MAGNA-TECH quick-change technology. The technology on the Anon goggles uses magnets for a seamless fit and allows riders to change out their lenses quickly and with only one hand if they so choose.

Women on the Rise

Burton created a full line of snowboards and equipment specifically for girls and women. Approximately 30 to 35 percent of snowboarders in the United States are female. As a result, snowboards designed for women such as the Hideaway Flat Top and Yeasayer Flat Top grew in popularity too. The women's versions of the Hometown Hero and Flying V boards were also popular.

The RISE

Olympic gold medalist Kelly Clark and Burton co-CEO Donna Carpenter worked together to release one of the most prized Burton women's boards in 2019. The RISE, a limited edition snowboard, was designed and produced in Vermont. It was made after Clark retired from competitive snowboarding following the 2018 Olympic Winter Games. Only 50 of these boards were made.

The Hideaway board was created in collaboration with members of Burton's women's team riders. It has a twin shape, which means it is symmetrical all around and the nose and tail of the board are the same. That helps with balance and makes it fun for a snowboarder to go in different directions. It also creates a lot of stability when people are riding the slopes. This board is perfect for beginners who are just learning the sport.

The Yeasayer is known for performing particularly well on mountainous terrain. The twin-tip design offers strong control. The board's graphics were inspired by opposite pairings such as darkness and light. It was created after design meetings with female snowboarders.

The Hometown Hero snowboards are designed to maneuver different terrains and conditions. Glass is strategically integrated into the board, which helps to make the nose and tail more rigid. This helps with control. Another popular board, the Feelgood Flying V, was endorsed by Kelly Clark. After its release in 1996, the board became a dominant force in

BURTON

#APRÈSINMAY

Listening to athletes has allowed Burton to create innovative snowboards.

women's snowboarding for two decades. Burton suggests the board as one for aspiring professionals or riders who "demand every advantage."

Chapter Four

OLYMPICS AND THE BURTON TEAM

S nowboarding took off in a powerful way in the 1990s. The sport joined the Olympic program for the first time in 1998 in Nagano, Japan. And when the Winter Games came to Salt Lake City in 2002, Burton was a name already associated with the boards worldwide.

Professional snowboarders had already made Burton's name widely known. American snowboarders Kelly Clark and Shaun White were among the early standouts who used Burton snowboards. Clark won the half-pipe gold medal in 2002. White made his Olympic debut four years later, winning a gold

Ross Powers won the bronze medal in men's half-pipe at the 1998 Olympics in Nagano, Japan.

medal in men's half-pipe. Over four more Olympics, he won an additional two gold medals. The two athletes partnered with Burton at the start of their careers. Both designed their own boards. However, White stepped away from Burton in 2022 to create his own brand of boards.

While many Olympians use Burton snowboards, the company has also designed Olympic team uniforms. The US snowboarding team wore Burton uniforms for the fourth time in 2018.

The Burton Team includes professional snowboarders who have competed in the World Cup circuit and other international tours.

Burton Ambassadors

In addition to the Burton Team, the company introduced the Burton Ambassadors to the world in 2020. This pulled together a group of everyday riders and social media influencers. The company explained that the ambassadors would represent a diverse group of "legends, activists, creators, and community leaders." They would share their voices on the Burton websites and social media platforms. The company defines the Burton Ambassadors as people "who are dedicated to improving the places where they live, work, and play every day."

Two of these Burton Ambassadors are Mary Walsh and Christine Savage. Walsh and Savage cofounded the Beyond the Boundaries snowboard camp for women. Its goal is to get more women more comfortable and involved in the sport of snowboarding.

The Pro Team

Burton pays professional snowboarders from around the world to use and endorse its products. This helps support the athletes, while they bring visibility to the company.

Recent members of the Burton Team have included

Shaun White is one of the most well-known snowboarders in the world.

Anna Gasser of Austria used a Burton snowboard for her 2018 Olympic big air gold-medal performance in PyeongChang, South Korea.

Anna Gasser of Austria. Gasser is a high-flying big air boarder who won Olympic gold medals in 2018 and 2022. She was the first woman to ever complete a cab double cork. This is a trick involving a double somersault from a frontside switch. After mastering the double cork, she later completed triple corks.

Japanese snowboarder Ayumu Hirano was also named to the Burton Team. He won his first Olympic men's half-pipe medal at age 15 in Sochi, Russia, in 2014. Hirano is famous for landing three triple corks in the 2022 Olympics in Beijing, China.

Another addition to the team was Iceland native Ylfa Runarsdottir. She has appeared in the snowboarding trilogy *The Uninvited.* "Something that really speaks to me is Burton's goal of lifting women in the scene. I want to be a part of that," said Runarsdottir, who joined the Burton Europe Team in 2021.

Chloe Kim partnered with Burton for seven years, parting ways in 2020. Kim made Olympic history in 2018. She became the youngest female snowboarder to win an Olympic gold medal at age 17. Kim won another gold medal in the 2022 Beijing Olympics.

Red Gerard joined the Burton Team. He won a gold medal in slopestyle in his Olympic debut in 2018. Gerard was promoted by Burton as the "new standard for all-terrain mastery."

Chloe Kim poses with her first Olympic gold medal in 2018.

Inspiring Kimmy

Kimmy Fasani and Burton collaborated to make snowboarding history. Fasani was the first woman to land a double backflip in both a terrain park environment and a backcountry trail in powder snow in 2011. She signed a deal that year to become the face of Burton's AK line of high-performance snowboarding gear. Fasani has appeared on the cover of multiple snowboarding magazines and in films. She appeared in *One World*, a Burton Snowboards film.

When Fasani became pregnant in 2017, she called Burton CEO Donna Carpenter. Fasani wanted to continue snowboarding. She also wanted to retain her partnership with Burton. Carpenter told her, "Let's do this."

In 2021 Fasani was diagnosed with breast cancer.

Burton partnered with Kimmy Fasani, *left*, while she fought breast cancer in 2021. The brand even featured her cancer journey on its website.

Through her breast cancer journey, Burton was a big supporter. The company was one of several businesses that supported the Benchetler Fasani Foundation. The foundation was created "to provide a meaningful connection to the outdoors for those who have suffered loss or hardship, by experiencing the healing properties found only in nature."

Personal Connection

In building the sport of snowboarding, Jake Burton Carpenter connected with Burton snowboarders personally. Carpenter often watched Shaun White's Olympic performances.

In 2010 Carpenter went to Vancouver, British Columbia, to see White win his second Olympic gold medal. Carpenter had given White a snowboard and an endorsement deal at age seven. "He's like the cool dad of the sport," White said.

A sad day arrived for the Burton Snowboards family. On November 20, 2019, Jake Burton Carpenter died due to cancer. The following day, John Lacy, a Burton co-CEO, announced Carpenter's death to the company's employees. Carpenter was 65 years old.

Chapter Five

STEPPING INTO THE FUTURE

In the early 2010s, company founder Jake Burton Carpenter asked Burton's engineers to design a binding system. He hoped to create new bindings that would make the sport more accessible to beginner riders. The project took five years of research and development as well as feedback from riders. Burton Step On bindings and boots made their debut in 2017.

The Step On system created boots that could be anchored to the binding without straps. Instead, each boot has three locking points: two near the toes and one on the heel. The locking points secure the boot

Burton Step On bindings are designed to make it easy for people to take their snowboards on and off.

Burton's Step On system meant that people had to buy Burton boots in order to use the snowboard.

to the binding. A release lever on the heel unlocks the boots from the binding.

This system allows riders to quickly snap into and out of their boards. They do not need to bend over or sit down to strap the board on or off. Before a run, the rider simply needs to step onto the board and make sure the locking points are engaged. However, the Step On binding system cost more than traditional boots and bindings. This was because both the Step On boots and Step On bindings must be purchased. The Step

On system did not work with standard boots.

Listening to snowboarders has been a part of Burton's game plan since the company's early years. The move toward Step On was no different. Riders reported that the Step On bindings created more power and precision than traditional bindings. However, the new system still had its criticisms. In a review for Snowboarder.com just before the new product became public, a reviewer didn't like the clicking noise that happened while turning. The reviewer also didn't like that the Step On system couldn't be used with other boots and bindings.

Burton instructed new Step On users to try the product at home before heading to the skiing and snowboarding hills. The guidelines called users to press their heel into the back of the boot and wait for a click. They then press down harder and wait for a second click. Users were then told to apply pressure with their toes. At that point, both cleats would lock into place. The company describes this process as "Heel. Toe. Go."

Snow Days

What's a snowboarding company to do when there is a big snowstorm? When a storm delivered at least two feet (0.6 m) of snow, Jake Burton Carpenter gave his employees the day off and told them to enjoy some snowboarding. In another way to enhance the work culture at Burton, he also encouraged staff members to bring their dogs to work.

Beginners' Guide

Getting people into snowboarding was important to the success of Burton. In order to help beginning snowboarders get started, the company has a "Snowboarding for Beginners" guide on its website. Snowboarding can seem like a scary sport to get into, so the guide answers a range of questions. It also explains the fun of the sport, what equipment to purchase, and whom to ride with.

The guide provides details on the sport and how to participate. It is ideal for beginners of all ages. The guide also includes a look at where to snowboard.

The Burton guide suggests consulting its list of global ski areas and resorts to see if the location is a good fit for a beginner. They can see answers to frequently asked questions to assess whether the resort is a suitable fit for their skill levels. Some of the questions pertain to the price of a lift ticket and

The Bernie Sanders Jacket

On January 20, 2021, crowds of people were gathered in Washington, DC. They were there to watch Joe Biden get sworn in as president of the United States. Most in attendance wore formal overcoats to keep warm. But one politician stood out. Bernie Sanders, a senator from Vermont, sat bundled up in bulky mittens. He also wore a stylish Burton snowboarding jacket. Sanders's look spread around the internet quickly through memes and social media posts.

snowboard rentals. Beginners can also learn whether there are lessons available. Providing this information can help people determine if the resort suits their needs.

Controversy of Love

Throughout Burton's history, the company has not had many controversies. But in 2008 Burton's Love snowboard line included images of nude women. A Primo snowboard included graphic images of bodily injury. Advocates for women and youth said the boards were inappropriate. Burton defended the boards as being forms of artistic expression. The Love snowboards featured images of models with little to no clothing. Employees at Vail Resorts in Colorado were not allowed to use the boards while on duty at work.

Donna Carpenter was not originally in favor of seeing these models on Burton boards. But after seeing the boards

Celebrities such as Emma Roberts have used Burton snowboards.

upon completion, Carpenter thought they were tasteful. She said young women liked the boards and purchased them worldwide.

The Final Word

Burton has been an innovator in the snowboarding world since its beginning in a Vermont barn. It receives stellar reviews on numerous websites. Its snowboards are tested and reviewed by experts. Mike Leighton of Curated.com was able to test a 2023 Burton Custom Camber at Powder Mountain in Utah. Leighton was impressed with the board's performance. He said, "There's a reason you saw this board in the most recent Olympics. There were multiple riders riding this in everything from slopestyle to half-pipe."

The company has built a dedicated customer following. Many of its specialty boards and clothing sell out. And by 2019, the year of Jake Burton Carpenter's death, a company that began in a barn had transformed into a $700 million business.

Jake Burton Carpenter's legacy lives on through the Burton brand.

TIMELINE

1977

Jake Burton Carpenter founds Burton Boards, working out of a barn in Vermont.

1981

Carpenter moves his factory from Londonderry, Vermont, to Manchester, Vermont. The barn next to his first house becomes the new factory.

1983

Carpenter marries Donna Gaston in Connecticut. Donna Gaston becomes Donna Carpenter.

1985

Burton establishes a global presence with the creation of a European office and manufacturing facility in Innsbruck, Austria.

1986

Burton's snowboards and gear are on sale at more than 1,000 retail shops in the United States.

1992

Burton moves its office and headquarters to Burlington, Vermont. It has more than 100 employees.

1995

The Carpenters establish the Chill Foundation.

2006

Shaun White is sponsored by Burton in his first Winter Olympics in Torino. White continues to ride Burton boards until his final Winter Olympics in 2022, when he rides his own brand's board.

2016

Donna Carpenter is named CEO of Burton. Also, Jake Burton Carpenter and artist Jeff Koons release a snowboard called the Philosopher. The money from the sales of this snowboard go to the Chill Foundation.

2019

Jake Burton Carpenter dies in a Burlington hospital in November at the age of 65.

IMPORTANT PEOPLE

Donna Carpenter

Donna Gaston met Jake Burton Carpenter at a New Year's Eve party. They married, and Donna Carpenter would become Burton Snowboards' chief financial officer and then chief executive officer.

Jake Burton Carpenter

Jake Burton Carpenter was the founder of Burton Snowboards. He first began making snowboards in a barn at a house in Vermont. The business would grow into a company worth hundreds of millions of dollars.

Kelly Clark

Kelly Clark won an Olympic gold medal in half-pipe snowboarding in Salt Lake City in 2002. She endorsed Burton Snowboards her entire career and worked with Burton and Donna Carpenter to release a limited edition RISE snowboard.

Kimmy Fasani

Kimmy Fasani worked with Burton to become the face of their AK line of high-performance gear. She appeared in magazines and Burton Snowboards' film *One World*. Fasani was also the first woman to land a double backflip in both a terrain park environment and a backcountry trail in powder snow.

Hermann Kapferer

Hermann Kapferer helped the Carpenters set up the first Burton office and manufacturing facility in Europe. The site in Innsbruck, Austria, became the start of Burton Europe.

Craig Kelly

Craig Kelly was known as one of the best freeriders in the world. He died in an avalanche in 2003 while training to become a Canadian mountain guide. Kelly was a close friend of Jake Burton Carpenter, and a Burton jacket and shirt were designed in his honor.

Chloe Kim

Burton signed Chloe Kim on as an endorser of the company's products as a teenager. She was riding a Burton board when she became the youngest female snowboarder to win an Olympic gold medal when she won the women's half-pipe event at age 17.

Shaun White

Shaun White won three Olympic gold medals in men's half-pipe, all while riding Burton snowboards. He formed an endorsement deal with Burton at the age of seven.

GLOSSARY

activists
People who strongly and publicly support one side of an issue.

binding
The part of a snowboard to which a boarder attaches his or her boots.

caretaker
A person who is taking care of a house or other building for the property owner.

endorse
To promote a company in exchange for their products or money.

freerider
A snowboarder who rides on all terrain types, especially in the backcountry.

innovative
New or trendy.

patent
To legally gain the exclusive right to make or sell a product.

prototype
An example of a product that is shown and worked on before it is ready to go on sale to the public.

ski resort
A recreational facility that is usually located in a mountainous area and hosts snowboarding and skiing on snowy trails.

terrain park
An outdoor park that has places for snowboarders and skiers to show off their tricks on difficult ground such as hills, bumps, and ramps.

MORE INFORMATION

BOOKS

Hewson, Anthony, K. *Shaun White*. Minneapolis, MN: Abdo Publishing, 2019.

Kingston, Seth. *Snowboarding*. New York: PowerKids Press, 2022.

Loh, Stefanie. *Who Is Chloe Kim?* New York: Penguin Workshop, 2022.

ONLINE RESOURCES

To learn more about Burton, please visit **abdobooklinks.com** or scan this QR code. These links are routinely monitored and updated to provide the most current information available.

INDEX

ABOUT THE AUTHOR

Paul D. Bowker is a sports editor, Olympics writer, and children's book author who grew up in Massachusetts and is now living in Iowa. He has written about many Olympic snowboarders for TeamUSA.org.